Coloring Book

ANIMALS
of
ANTARCTICA

Mark Shawe

Book Series: Animal Planet

In this Coloring Book you will find:

- 20 original realistic full-page images of wild animals of Antarctica on single-sided sheets to prevent bleed-through
- 60 interesting unusual facts about the animals

Grab you favorite tool: pencils, crayons, markers or paints, and start coloring!

ISBN: 9781079225969

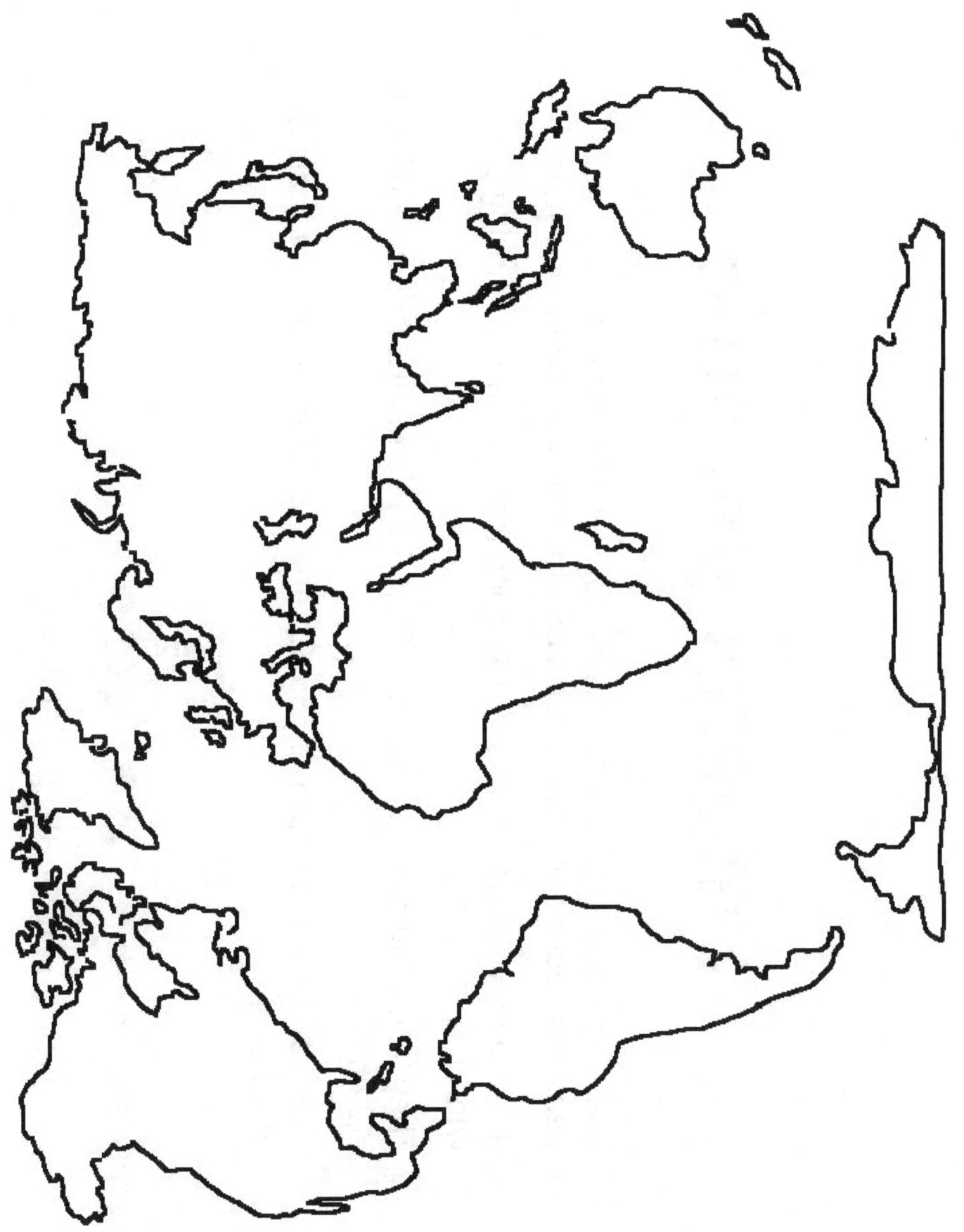

WORLD MAP

Emperor penguin

The emperor penguin is the largest species of penguins. Emperor penguins spend their entire lives on Antarctic ice and in its waters.

It is the only animal to inhabit the open ice of Antarctica during the winter.

They face wind chills as cold as -60°C (-76°F) and blizzards of 200 km/h (124 mph).

They can dive to a depth of 565 meters (1,870 feet) – deeper than any other bird.

life expectancy in nature

weigh up to   35 kg (77 lb)

23

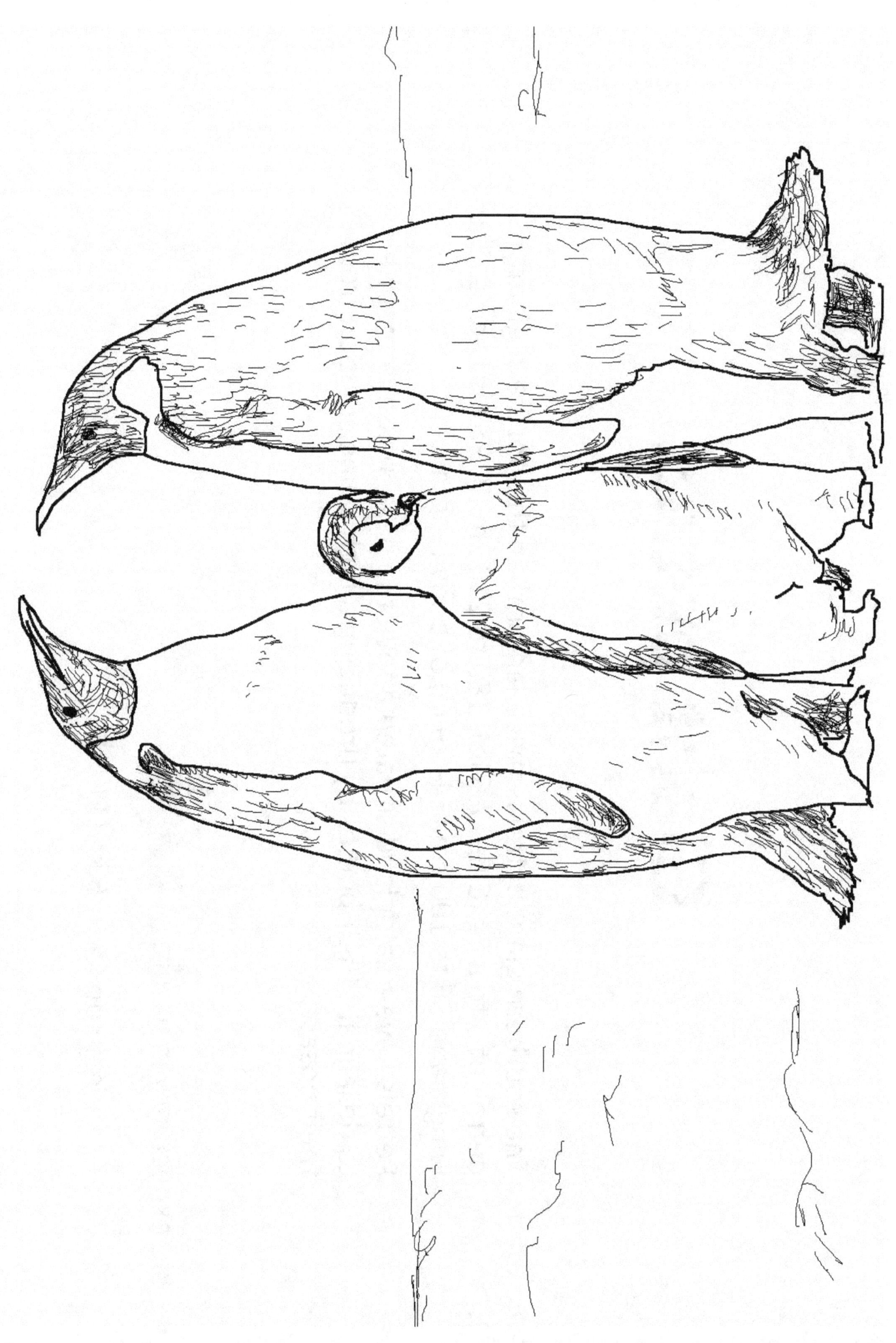

Giant petrel

The southern giant petrel is twice larger than the northern giant petrel, at 3 to 8 kg (6.6–17.6 lb), 180 to 210 cm (71–83 in) across the wings, and 86 to 100 cm (34–39 in) of body length.

Petrels have a salt gland situated above the nasal passage that helps to desalinate their bodies by producing a high saline solution from their noses.

.

life expectancy in nature

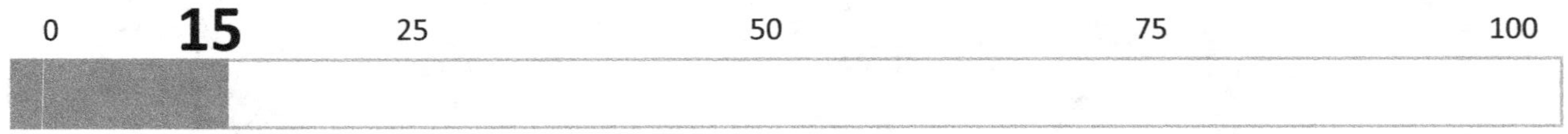

15

0   25   50   75   100

weigh up to   5 kg (11 lb)

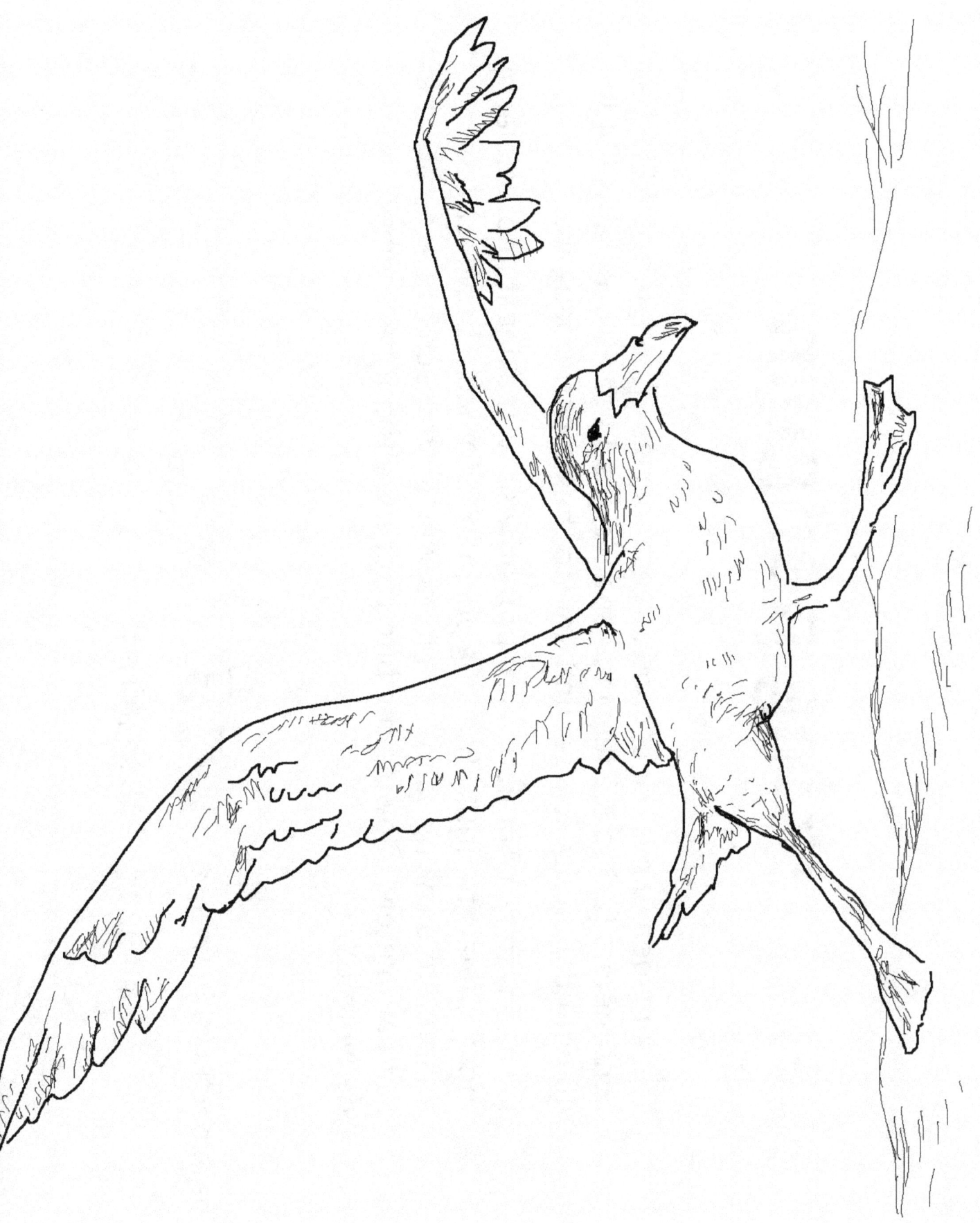

King penguin

The king penguin is the second largest species of penguin at 70 to 100 centimeters (2.3 to 3.2 feet) tall and weighs 11 to 18 kilograms (24 to 40 pounds). In size it is second only to the emperor penguin.

Ice and water in Antarctica are primarily salty, making it impossible for most animals to drink. The king penguin's stomach, however, has adapted to drinking salt water. Its powerful stomach can separate the salt completely, allowing the bird to drink without becoming dehydrated.

life expectancy in nature

0   **15**   25   50   75   100

weigh up to   18 kg (40 lb)

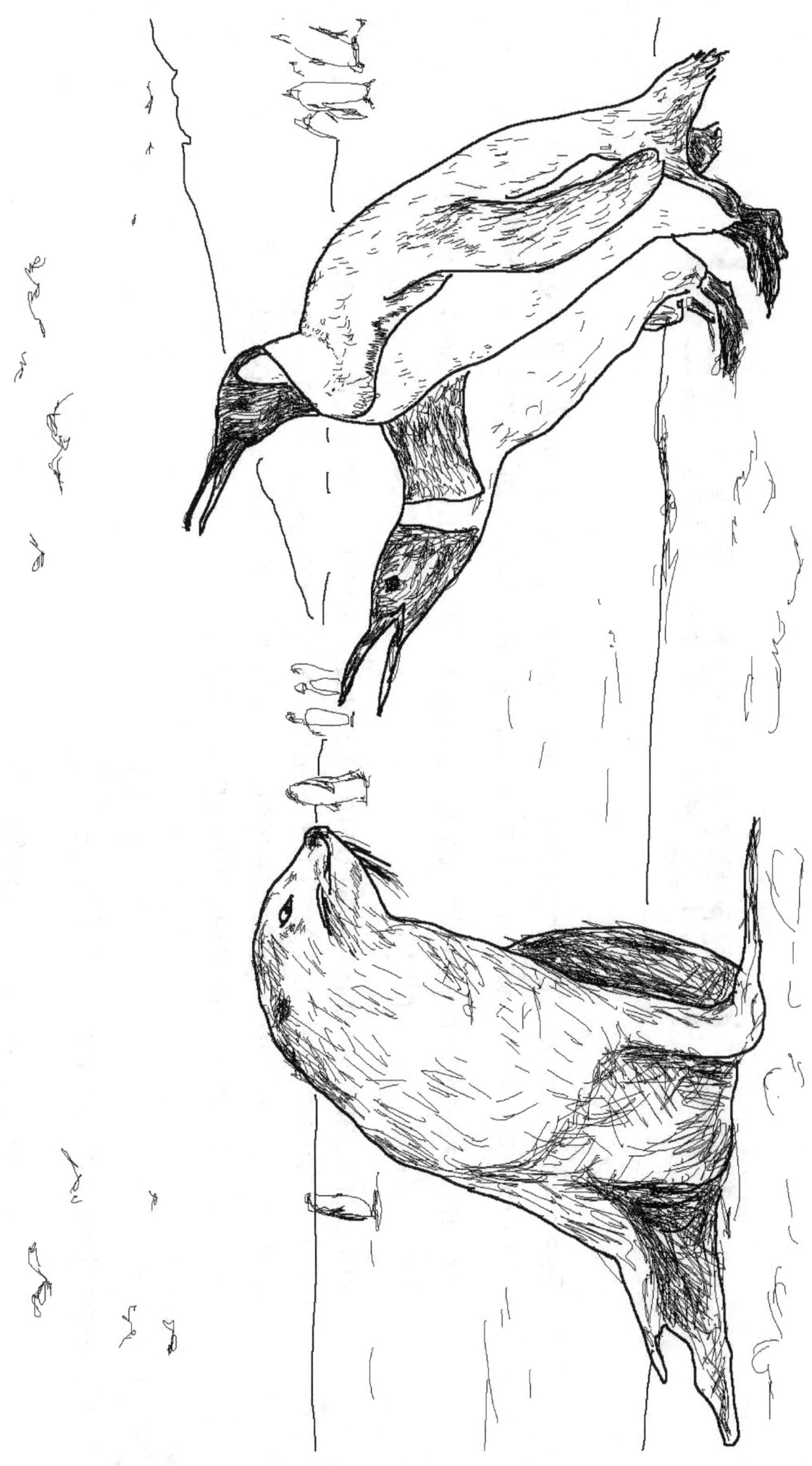

The Kerguelen fur seal

Seals have a well-developed sense of hearing, especially in the water. Their vision under water is better than a human's, but worse on land.

Adult seals can stay underwater for up to 30 minutes but dives usually last only about 3 minutes.

Harbor seals sleep on land or in the water. In the water they sleep at the surface and often assume a posture known as bottling – their entire bodies remain submerged with just their heads exposed. This enables them to breathe when necessary.

life expectancy in nature

23

0   25   50   75   100

weigh up to   200 kg (440 lb)

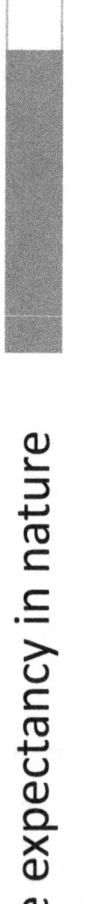

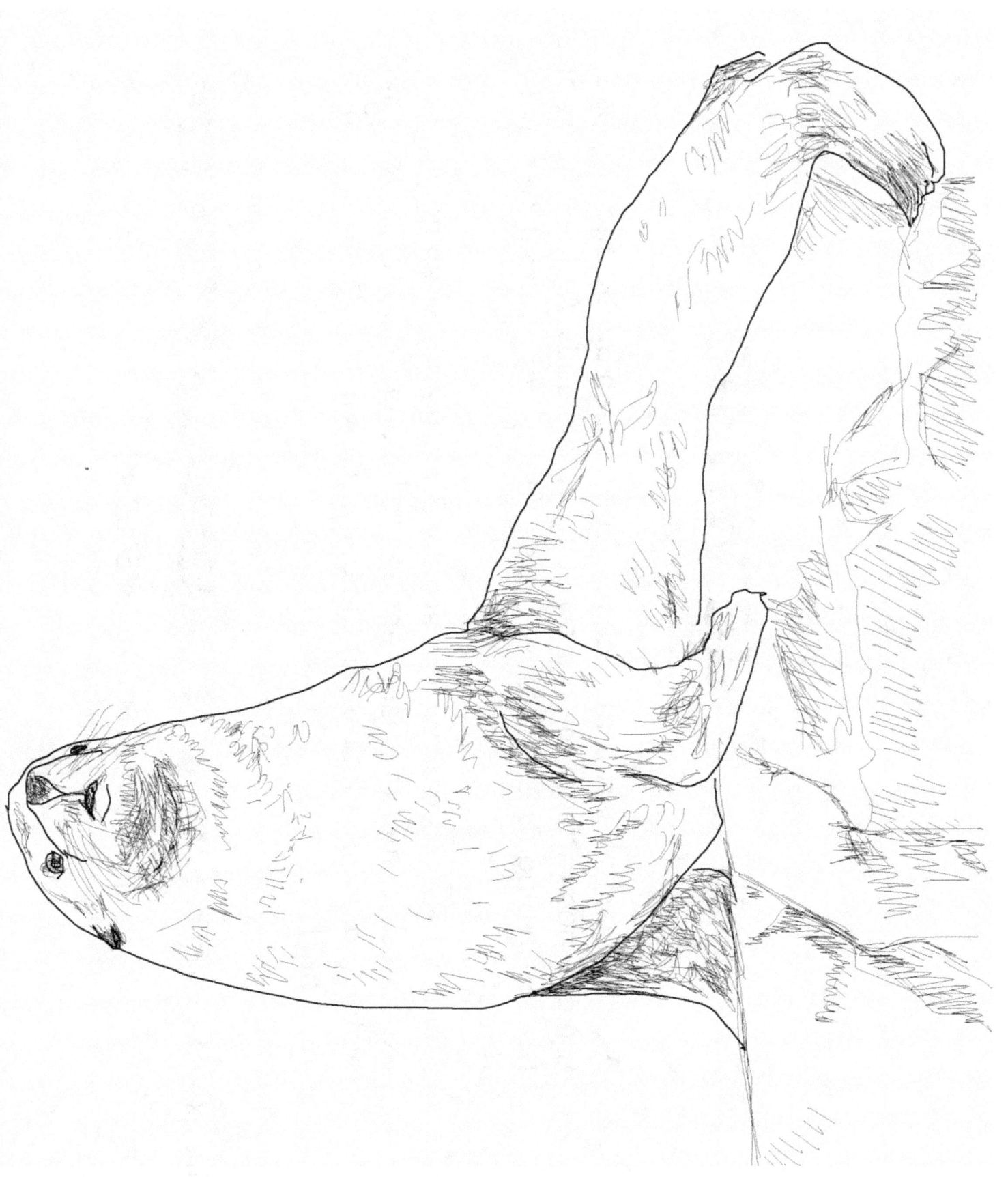

Blue whale

A blue whale's heart is the size of a Volkswagen Beetle and pumps 9 ton of blood through the massive blue whale body. A blue whale aorta (the main blood vessel) alone is large enough for a human to crawl through.

A blue whale's tongue weighs around 2.7 ton and, when fully expanded, its mouth is large enough to hold up to 90 ton of food and water. (So, Jonah's journey in the belly of a whale gotta be true, don't ya think?)

life expectancy in nature

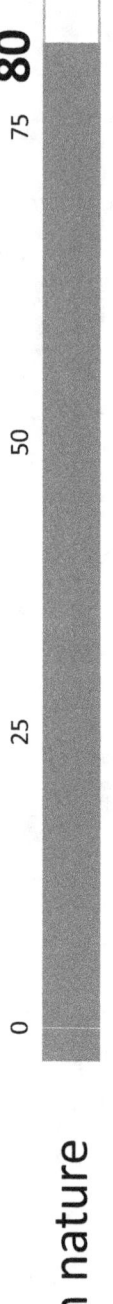

0   25   50   75   **80**   100

weigh up to   120000 kg (265000 lb)

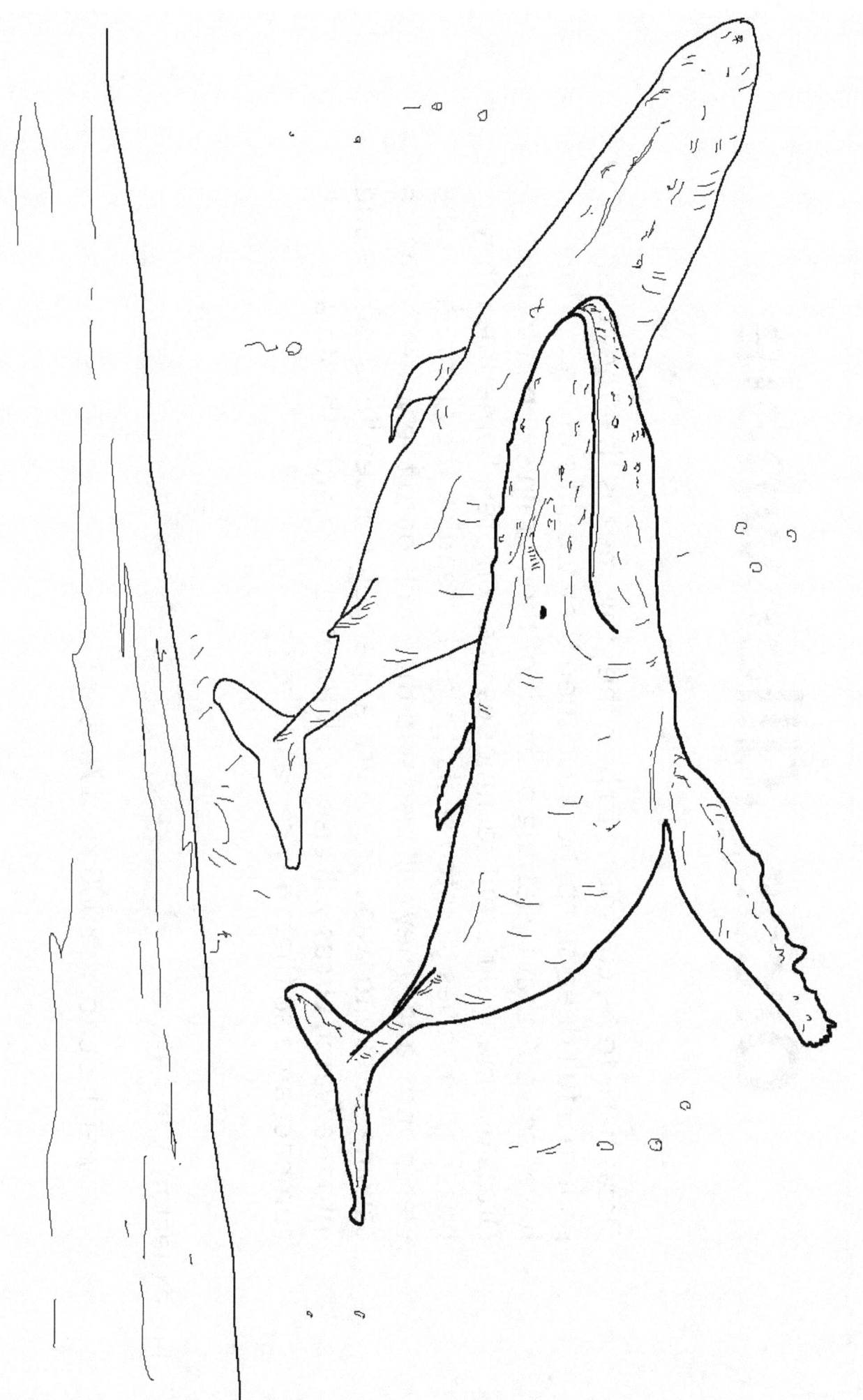

Orcas, Killer whale

Orcas have to be conscious to breathe. This means that they cannot go into a full deep sleep, because then they would suffocate. They have "solved" that by letting one half of their brain sleep at a time. Orcas use many different techniques to catch prey. Sometimes they beach themselves to catch seals on land, meaning they jump from the water onto land. They will also slap their tails onto the water's surface, causing a wave to wash prey, such as penguins or sea lions, off ice and into the water. Orcas will also work together to herd fish into a compact area so that they're easier to eat.

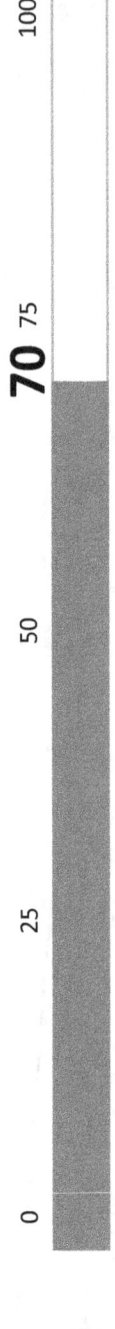

life expectancy in nature

0   25   50   70 75   100

weigh up to   8000 kg (17600 lb)

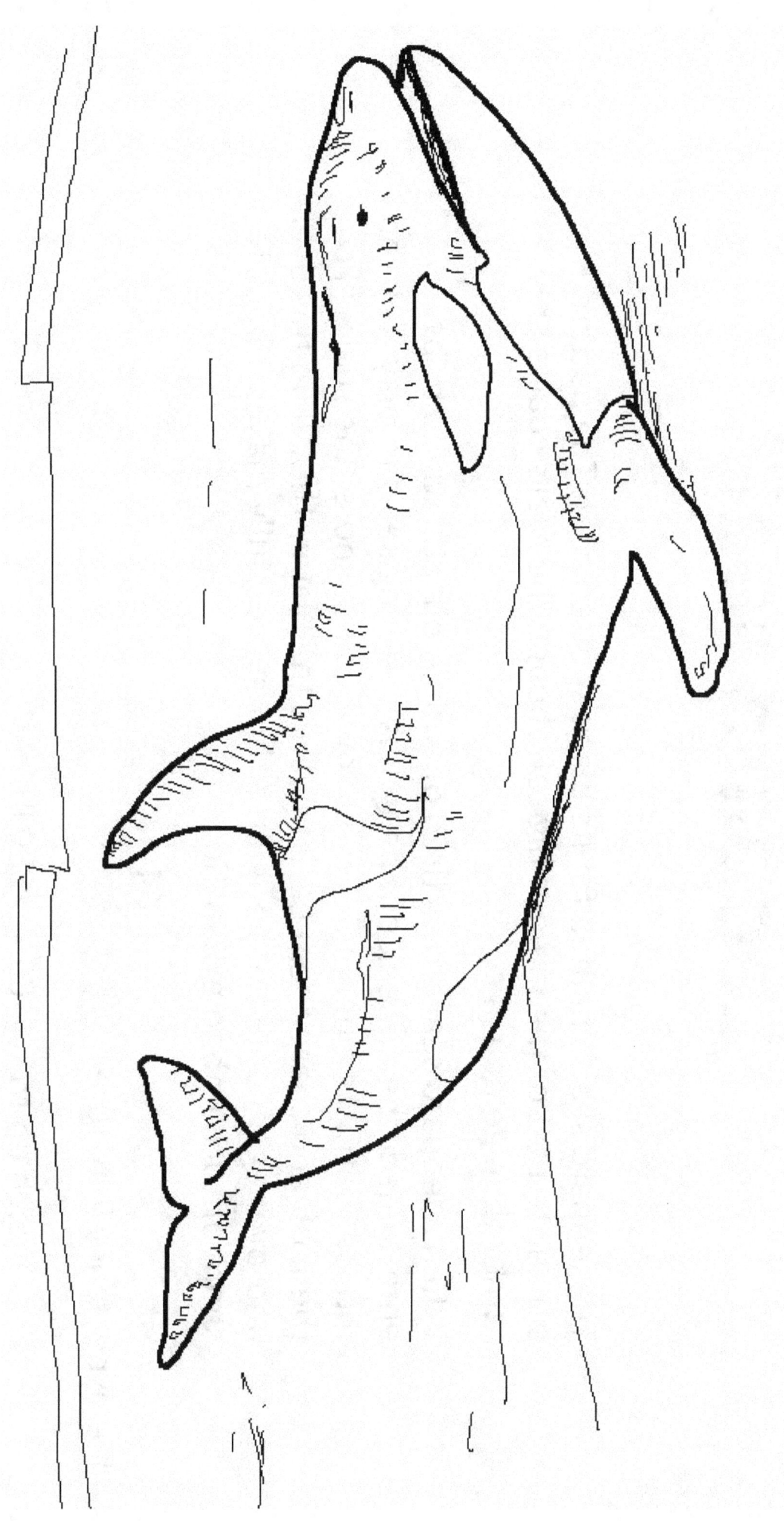

Leopard seal

The leopard seal is named for its black-spotted coat. The pattern is similar to that of the famous big cat, though the seal's coat is gray rather than golden in color.

When a leopard seal grows tired of eating, but still wants to be entertained, they'll seek out penguins or young seals to play "cat and mouse" with. As a penguin swims towards the shore, the seal will cut them off and chase them back towards the water. They'll do this over-and-over again until the penguin either successfully makes it back to shore or succumb to exhaustion.

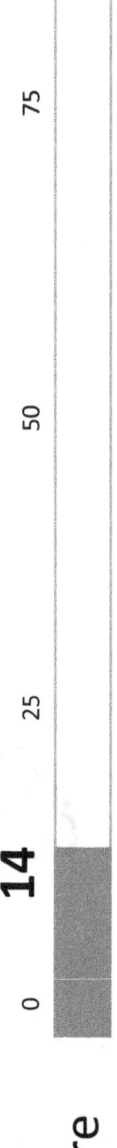

life expectancy in nature

0   **14**   25   50   75   100

weigh up to   400 kg (880 lb)

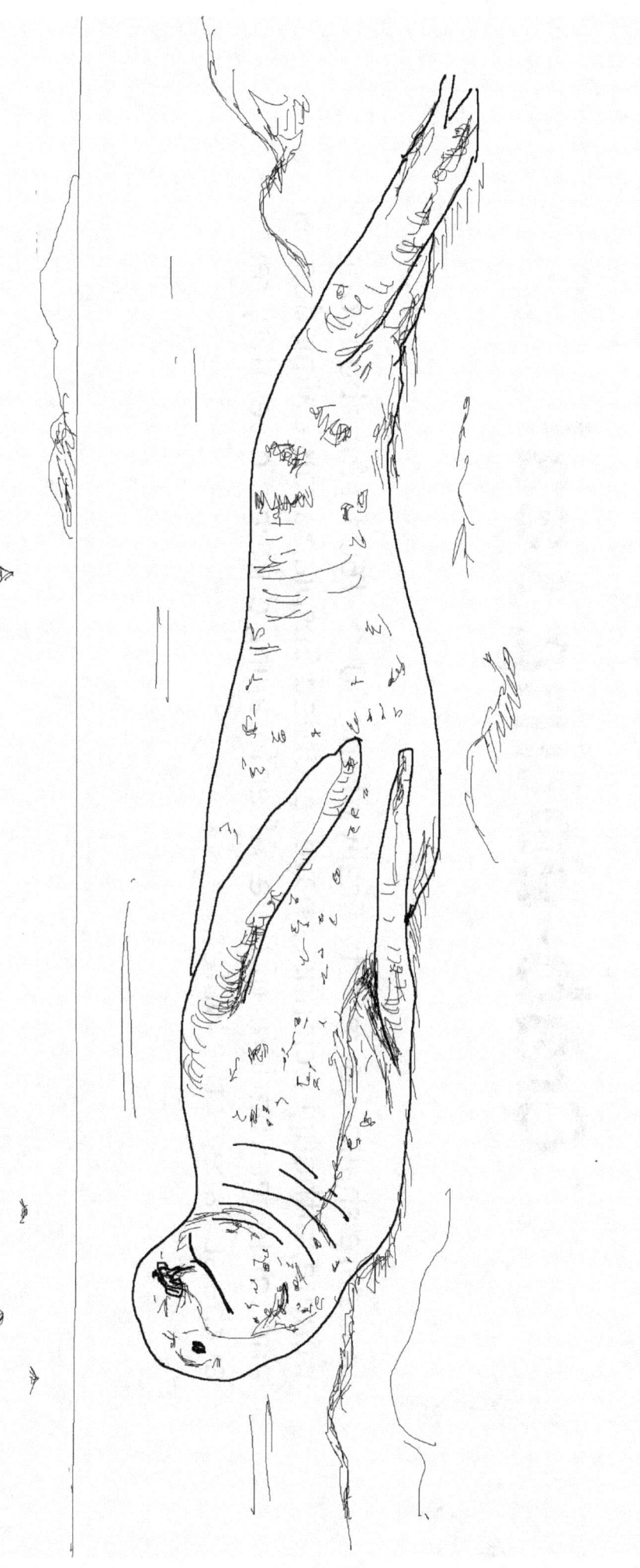

Crab-eating seal

Seals are shallow divers, typically diving 50 m (160 ft) for about one minute, although scientists have recorded Caspian seals diving deeper and for longer periods of time. After foraging during a dive, they rest at the surface of the water

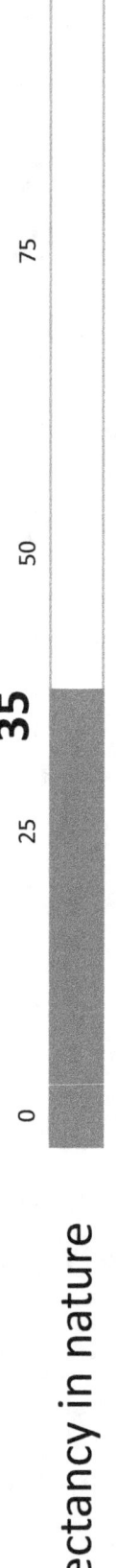

| | 0 | 25 | **35** | 50 | 75 | 100 |

life expectancy in nature

weigh up to   300 kg (650 lb)

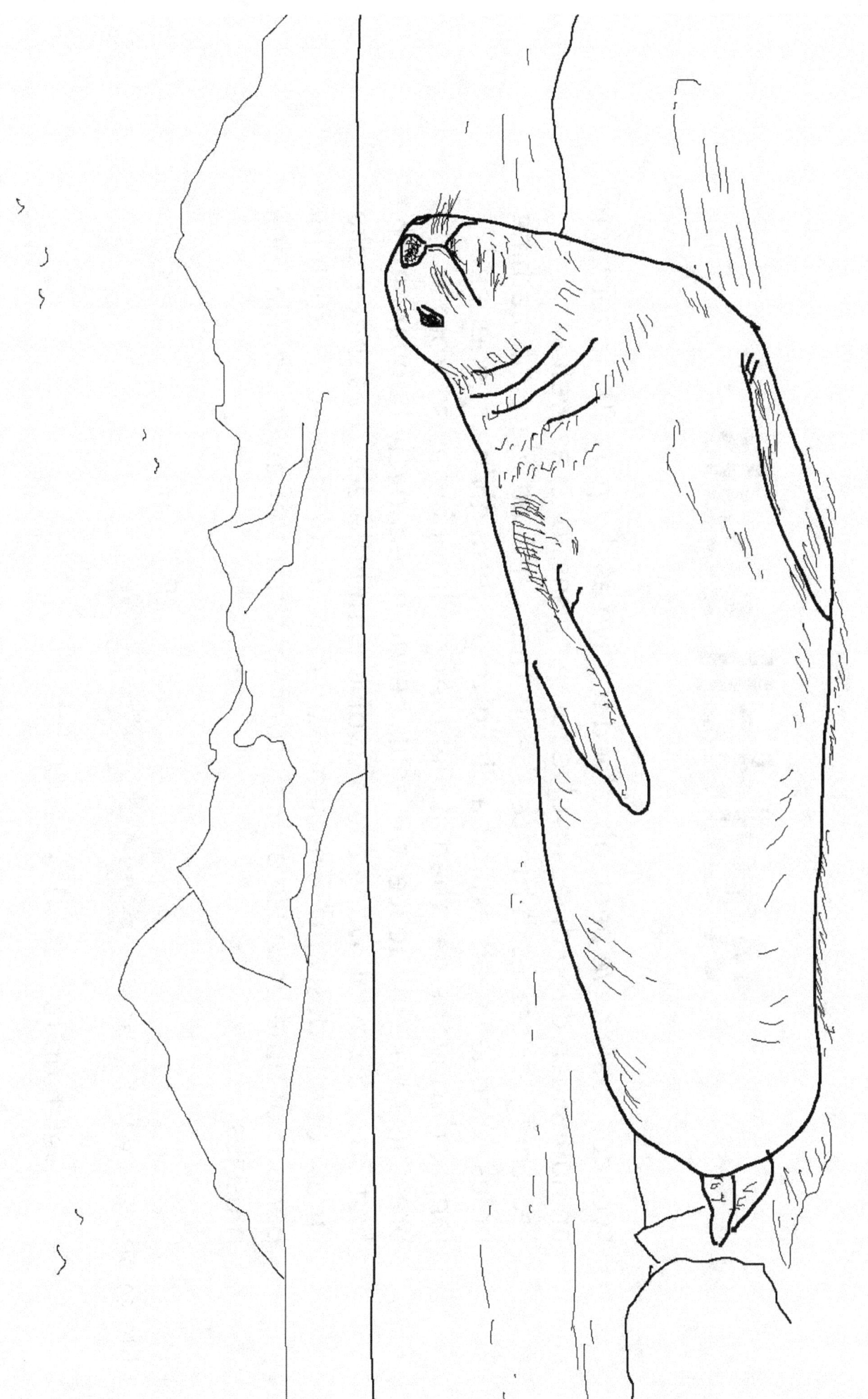

Weddell seals

Weddell seals have been observed to dive as deep as 600 m for up to an hour. Such deep dives involve foraging sessions, as well as searching for cracks in the ice sheets that can lead to new breathing holes. Weddell seals exhibit a diel dive pattern, diving deeper and longer during the day than at night. After dropping away from a breathing hole in the ice, the seals become negatively buoyant in the first 30 to 50 m, allowing them to dive with little effort as they make a "meandering descent". The seals can remain submerged for such long periods of time because of high concentrations of myoglobin in their muscles.

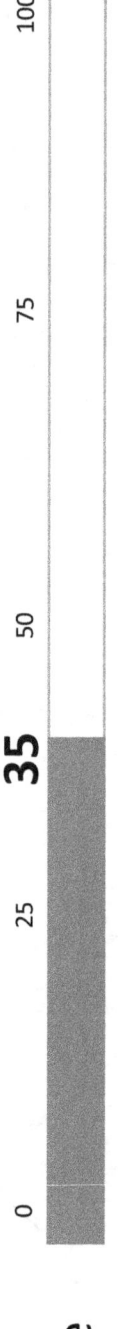

life expectancy in nature

weigh up to   450 kg (1000 lb)

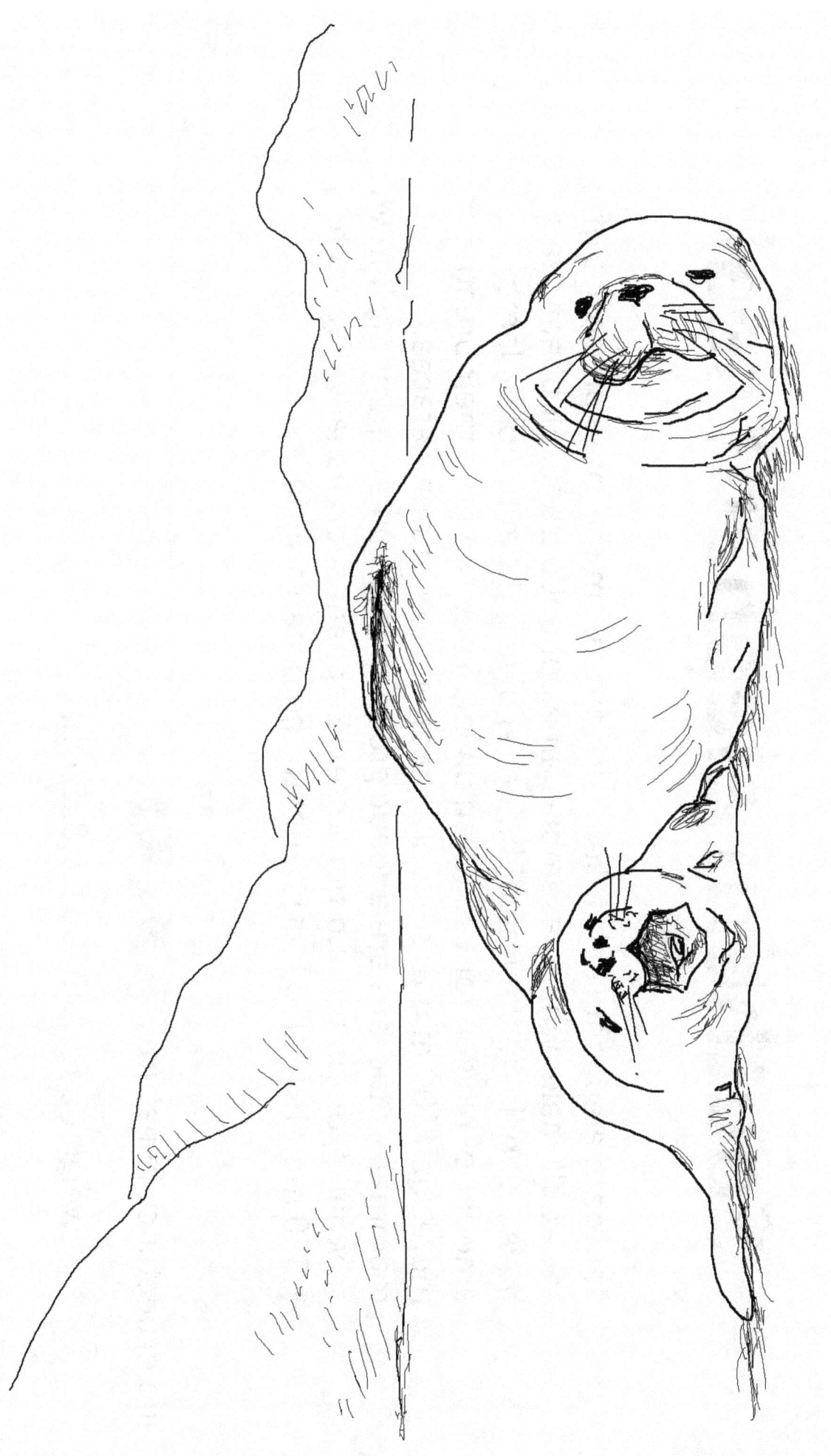

Southern elephant seal

Southern elephant seals take their name from the large proboscis of the adult male, which resembles an elephant's trunk. Elephant seals have a very large volume of blood, allowing them to hold a large amount of oxygen for use when diving. They can hold their breath for more than 100 minutes — longer than any other non-cetacean mammal. Cetaceans are aquatic group of mammals commonly known as whales, dolphins, and porpoises. Elephant seals usually dive up to 1,550 meters (5,090 feet) beneath the ocean's surface

life expectancy in nature

16

0   25   50   75   100

weigh up to   3700 kg (8150 lb)

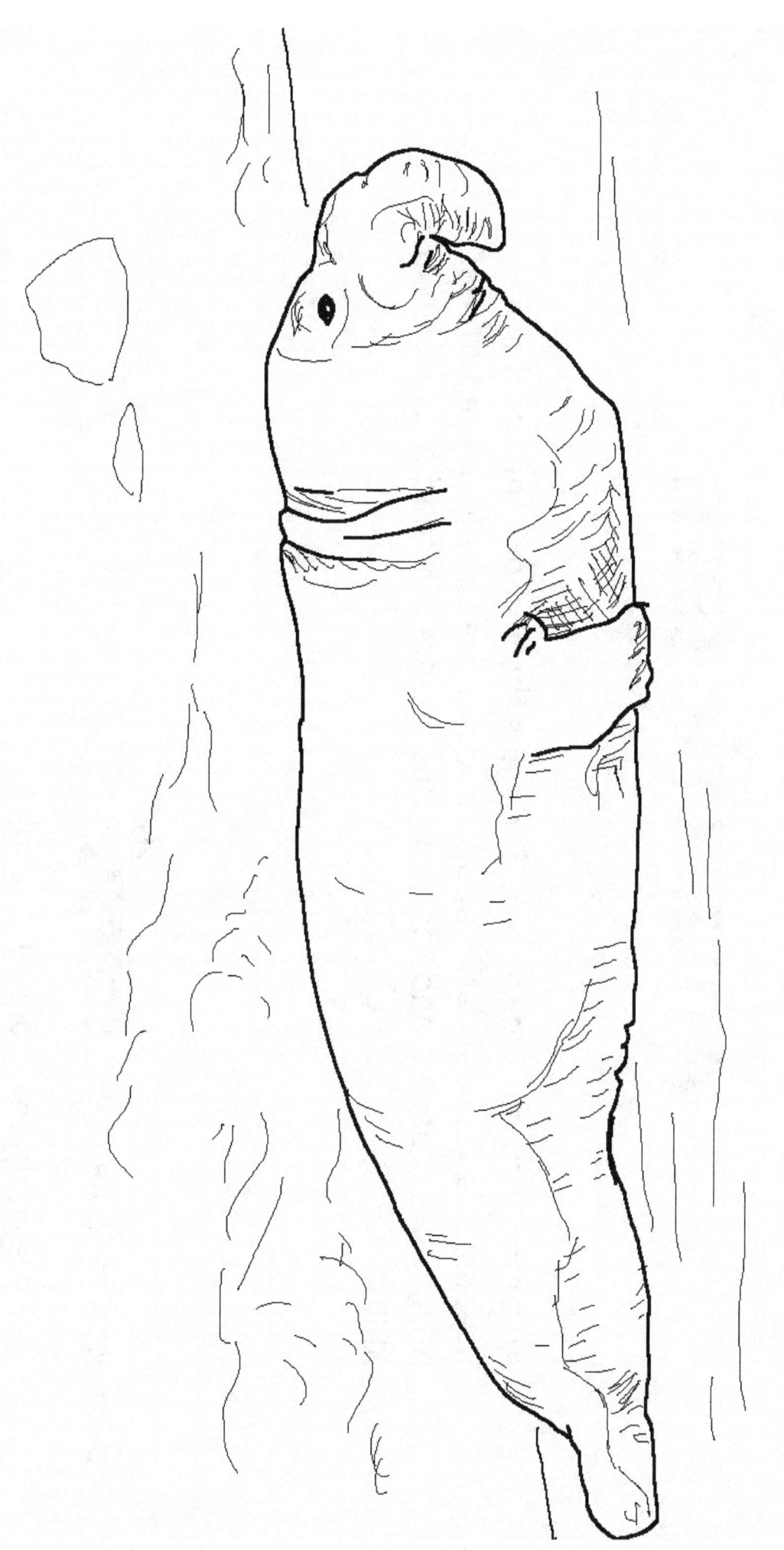

Antarctic tern

Antarctic tern is a typical tern. It ranges throughout the southern oceans. It is very similar in appearance to the closely related Arctic tern, but is stockier, and the wing tips are grey instead of blackish in flight.

life expectancy in nature

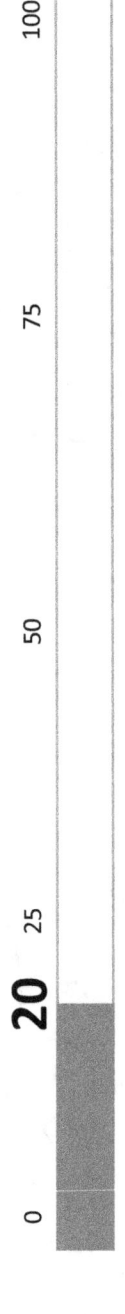

0   **20** 25   50   75   100

weigh up to   0,1 kg (0,2 lb)

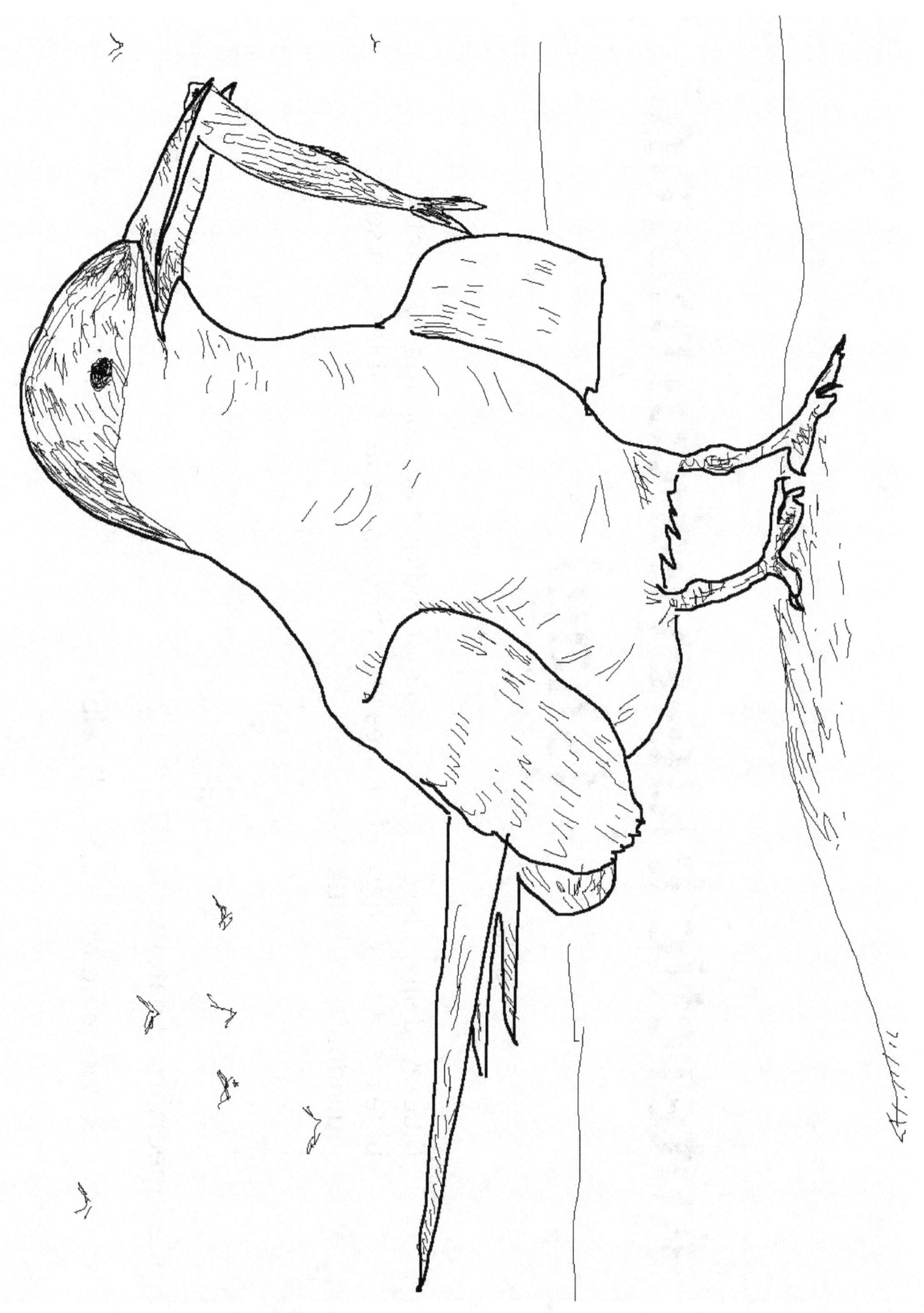

Antarctic blue-eyed cormorant (shag)

Blue-eyed shag have a blue, purple or red ring around the eye (not a blue iris); other shared features are white underparts (at least in some individuals) and pink feet

life expectancy in nature

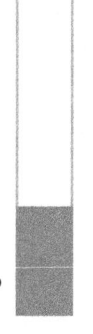

6

0   25   50   75   100

weigh up to   3,5 kg (7,7 lb)

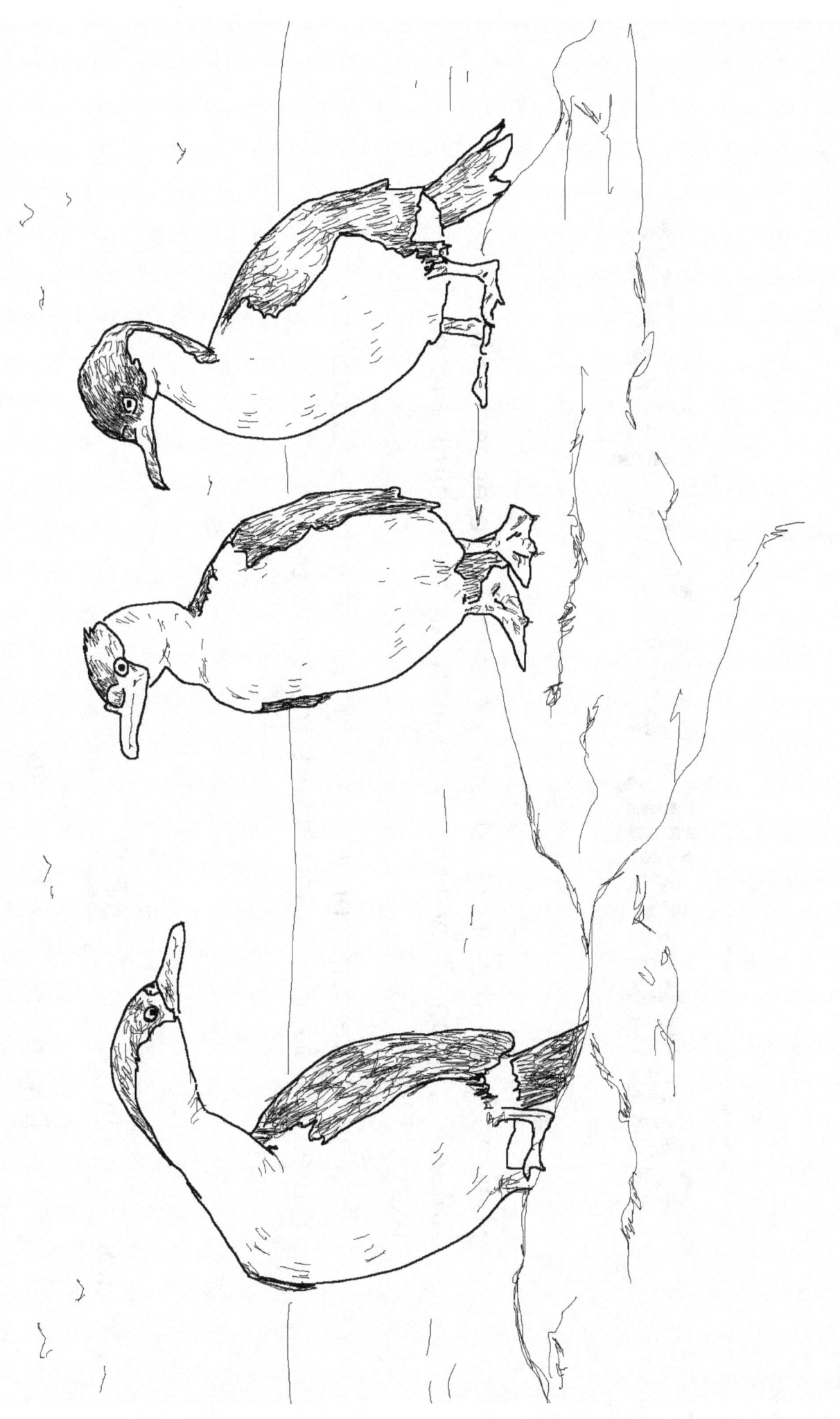

Sheathbill, White plover

Sheathbills are the only bird family endemic as breeders to the Antarctic region. They are also the only Antarctic birds without webbed feet.

Sheathbills are commonly known in the Antarctic as "Mutts" because of their call which is a soft "Mutt, mutt, mutt"

life expectancy in nature

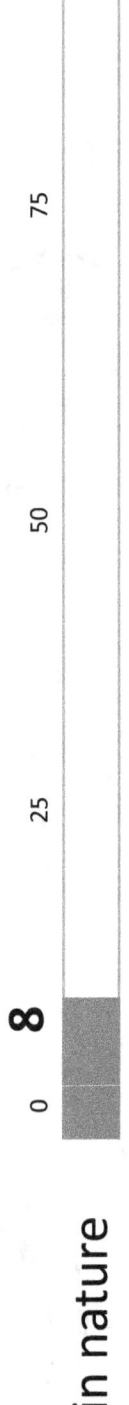

0   **8**   25   50   75   100

weigh up to   0,8 kg (1,7 lb)

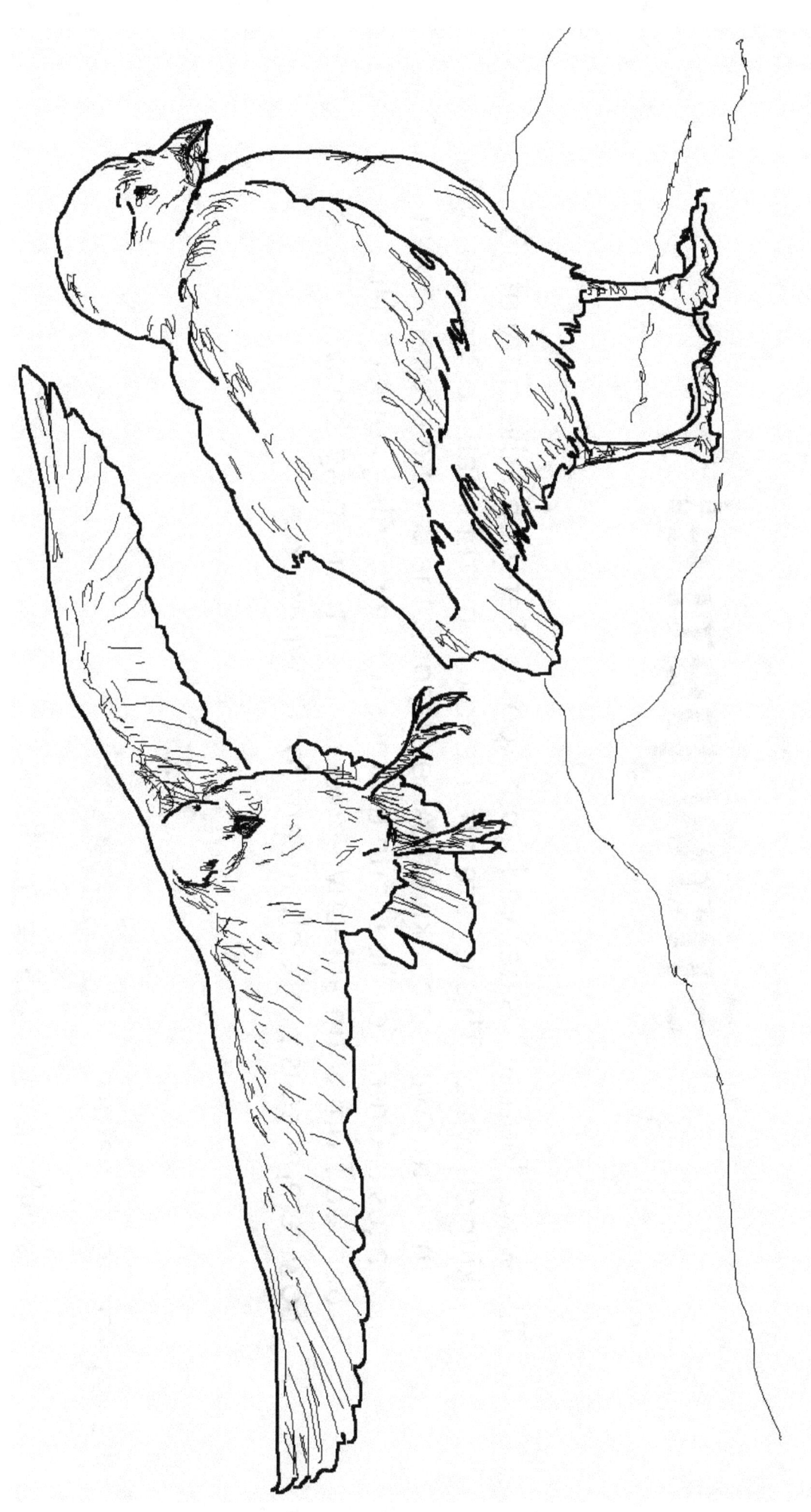

Snow petrel

The word "petrel""" is derived from Apostle Peter and the story of his walking on water. This is in reference to the petrel's habit of appearing to run on the water to take off. Also, Pagodroma can be broken down as, pagos is Greek for "ice" and dromos for "a running course". Nivea is derived from Latin adjective niveus, -a, -um meaning "snowy". The snow reference is probably meant for its white color.

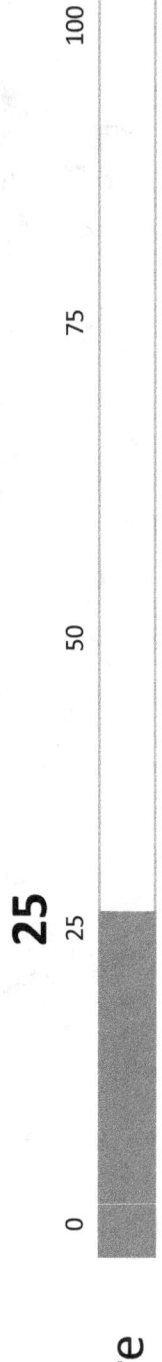

25

life expectancy in nature

weigh up to   0,5 kg (1,1 lb)

0   25   50   75   100

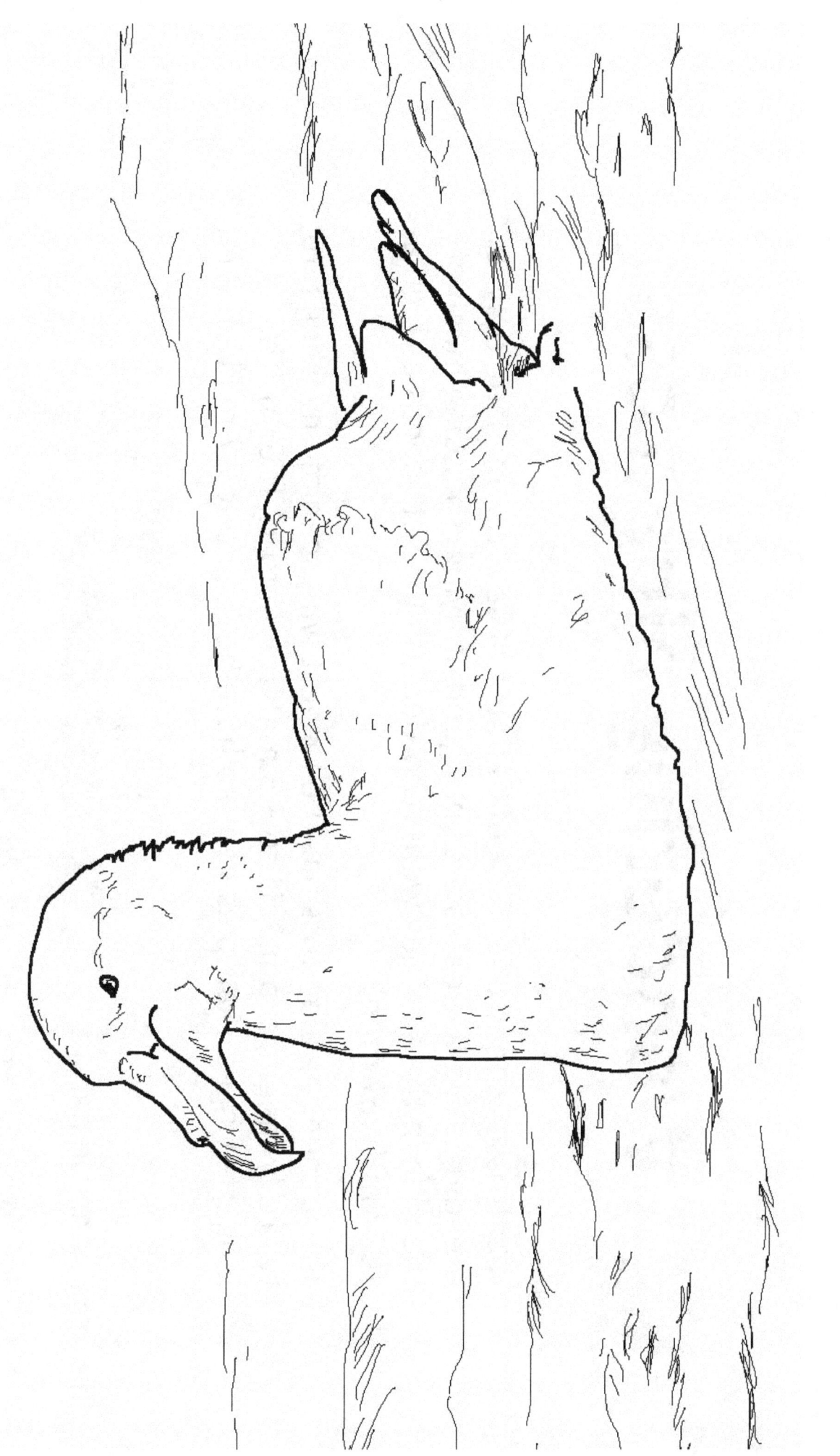

Wandering albatross

Albatrosses spend over 80% of their life at sea, visiting land only for breeding. All albatrosses are very good at flying, spending much of their life in the air. They were recorded as flying at speeds as high as 108 km/h (67 mph).

The wandering albatross has the longest wingspan of any living bird, typically ranging from 2.51 to 3.5 m (8 ft 3 in to 11 ft 6 in). The longest-winged examples verified have been about 3.7 m (12 ft 2 in)

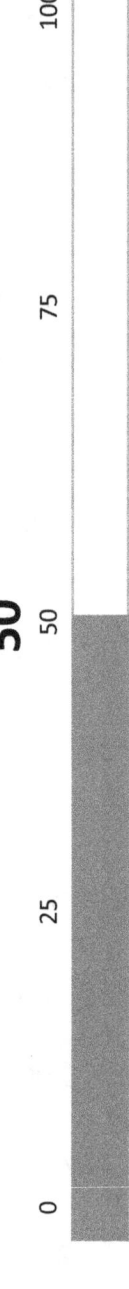

life expectancy in nature

weigh up to   12 kg (26 lb)

0   25   **50**   75   100

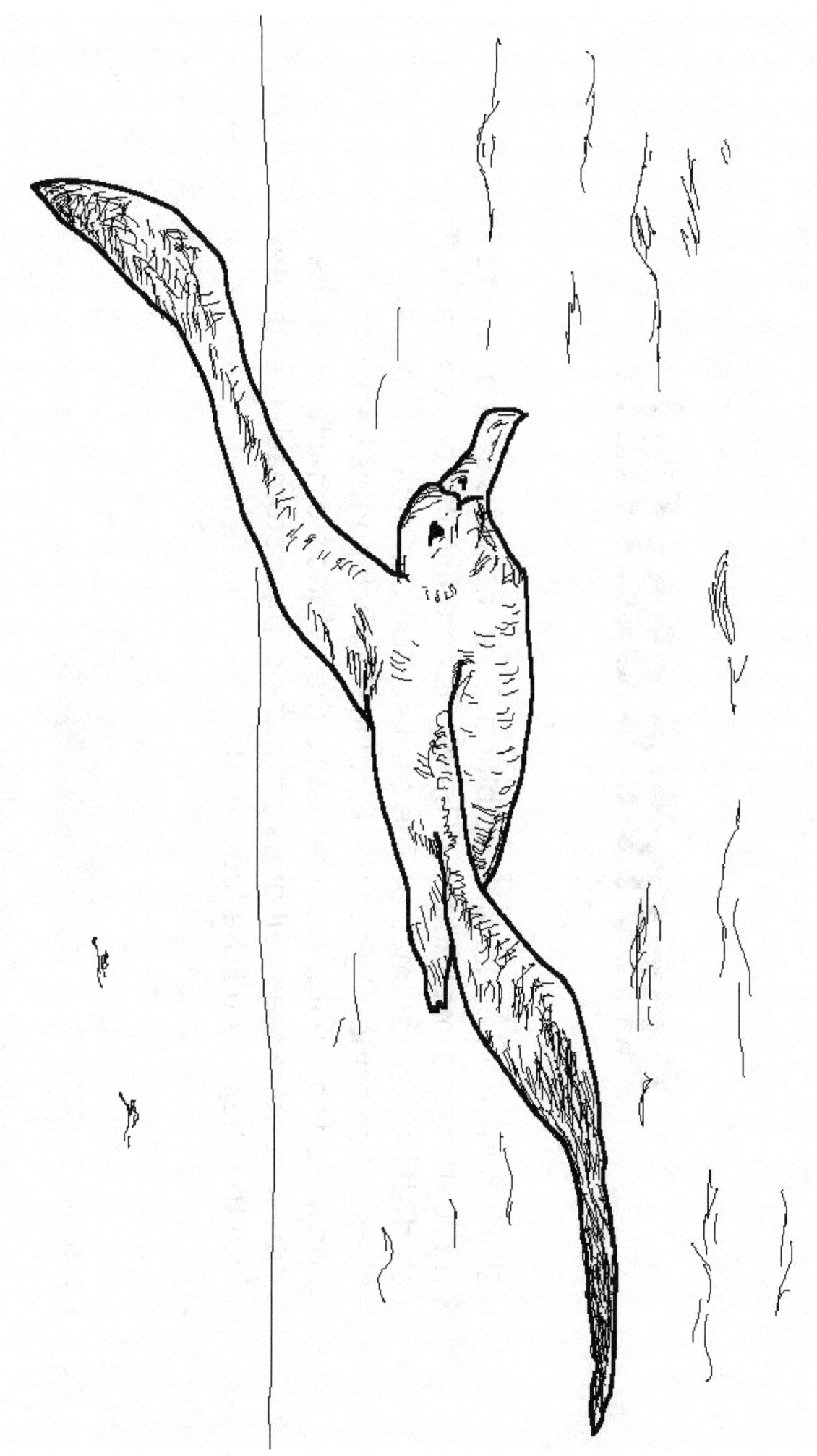

Antarctic starfish

Starfish have no brains and no blood. Their nervous system is spread through their arms and their "blood" is actually filtered sea water. The starfish has two stomachs. The cardiac stomach eats the food outside the starfish's body. When the cardiac stomach comes back into the body, the food in it is transferred to the pyloric stomach. After the tube feet open the shell of its prey, the cardiac stomach is extended into the shell to pull the food inside.

life expectancy in nature

0	25	**35**	50	75	100

weigh up to   0,6 kg (1,3 lb)

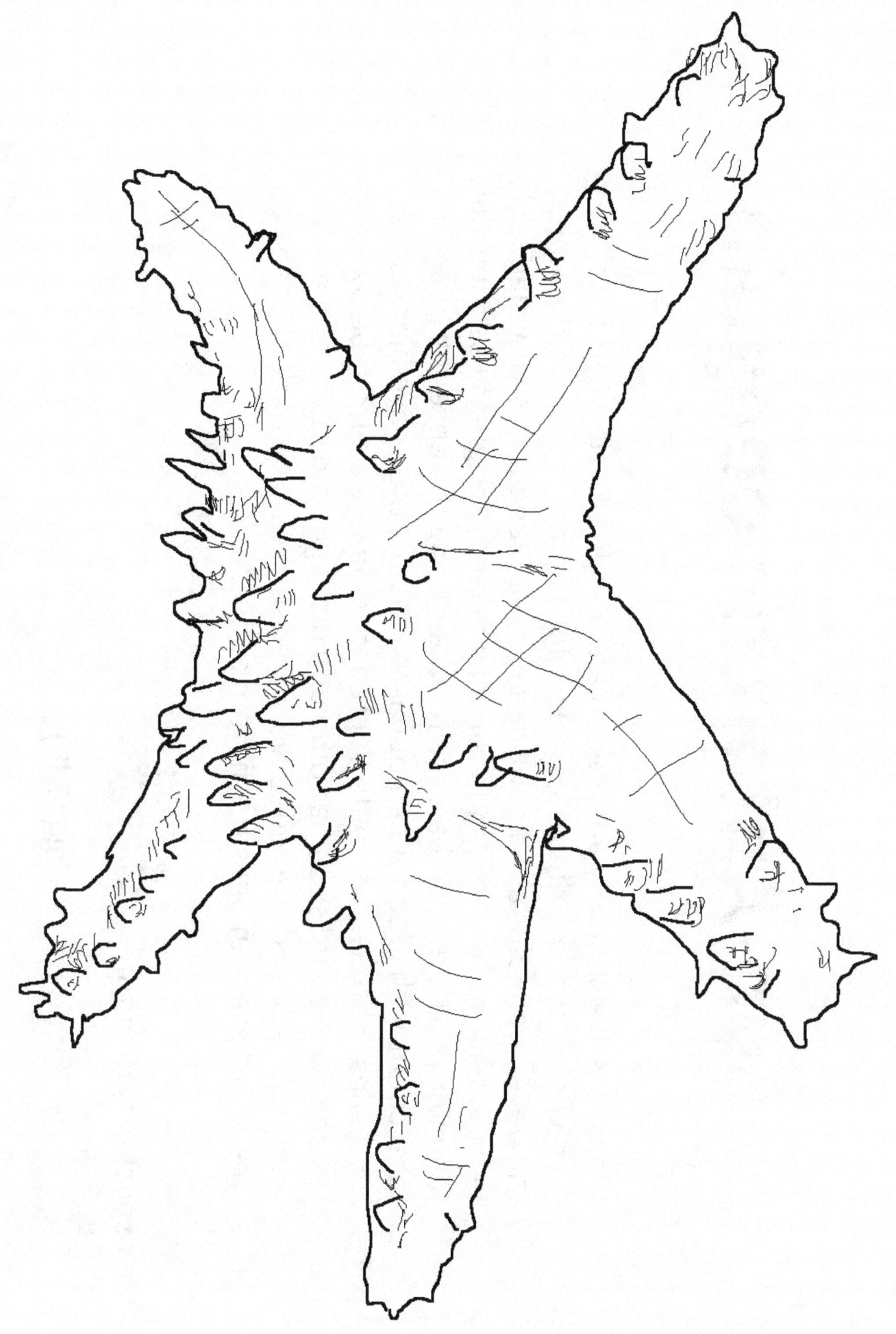

Sub-Antarctic penguin

Penguins are superbly adapted to aquatic life. Their wings have evolved to become flippers, useless for flight in the air. In the water, however, penguins are astonishingly agile. Penguins' swimming looks very similar to bird's flight in the air. On land, penguins use their tails and wings to maintain balance for their upright stance. All penguins are counter shaded for camouflage – that is, they have black backs and wings with white fronts. A predator looking up from below (such as an or a leopard seal) has difficulty distinguishing between a white penguin belly and the reflective water surface. The dark plumage on their back camouflages them from above.

life expectancy in nature

0	**13**	25	50	75	100

weigh up to   8 kg (17 lb)

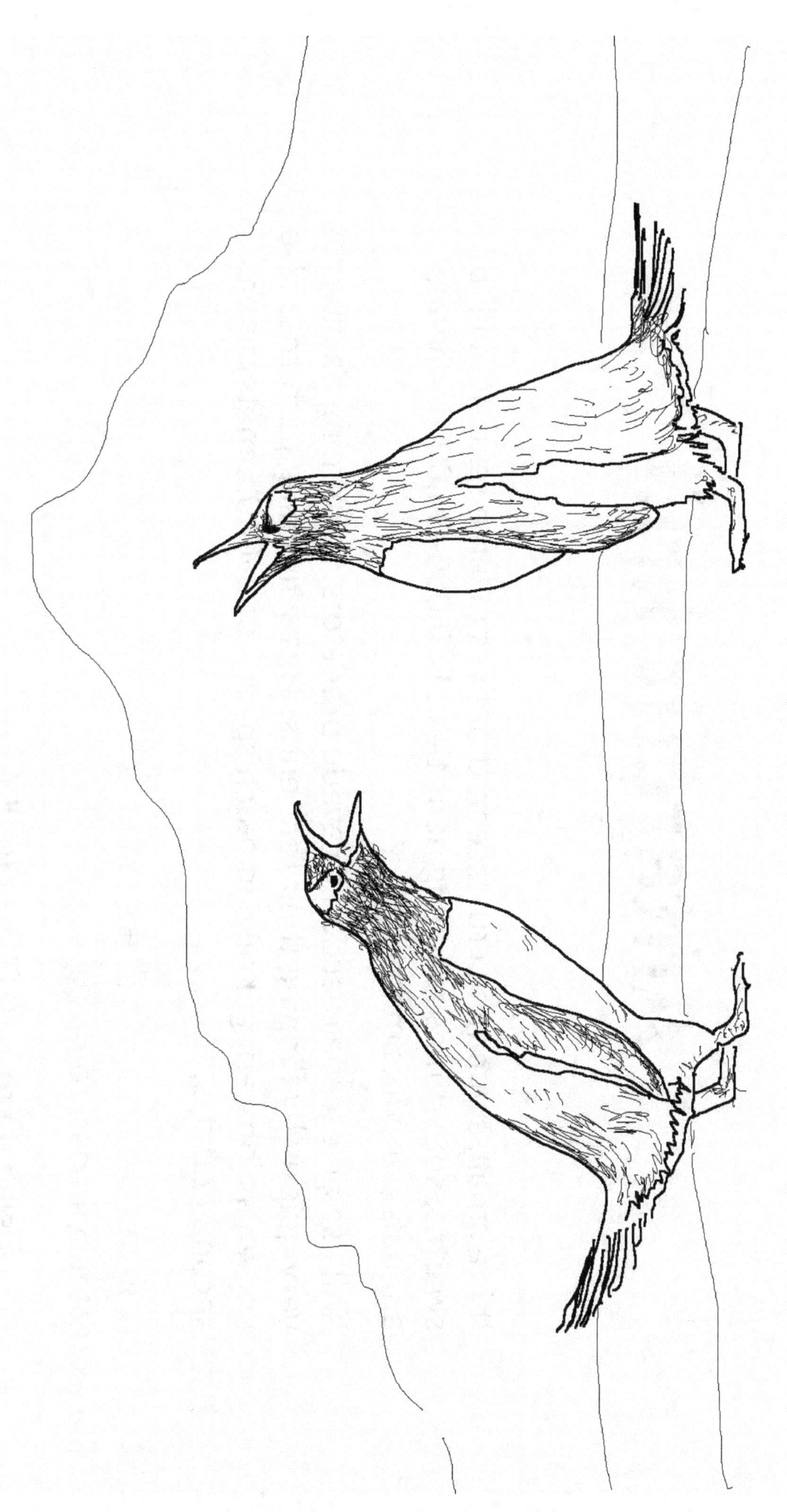

Antarctic krill

It is a small, swimming crustacean that lives in large schools, called swarms, sometimes reaching densities of 10,000–30,000 individual animals per cubic meter.

Krill use an escape reaction to evade predators, swimming backwards very quickly by flipping their rear ends. This swimming pattern is also known as lobstering. Krill can reach speeds of over 0.6 meters per second (2.0 ft/s)

4

| 0 | 25 | 50 | 75 | 100 |

life expectancy in nature

weigh up to   0,002 kg (0,004 lb)

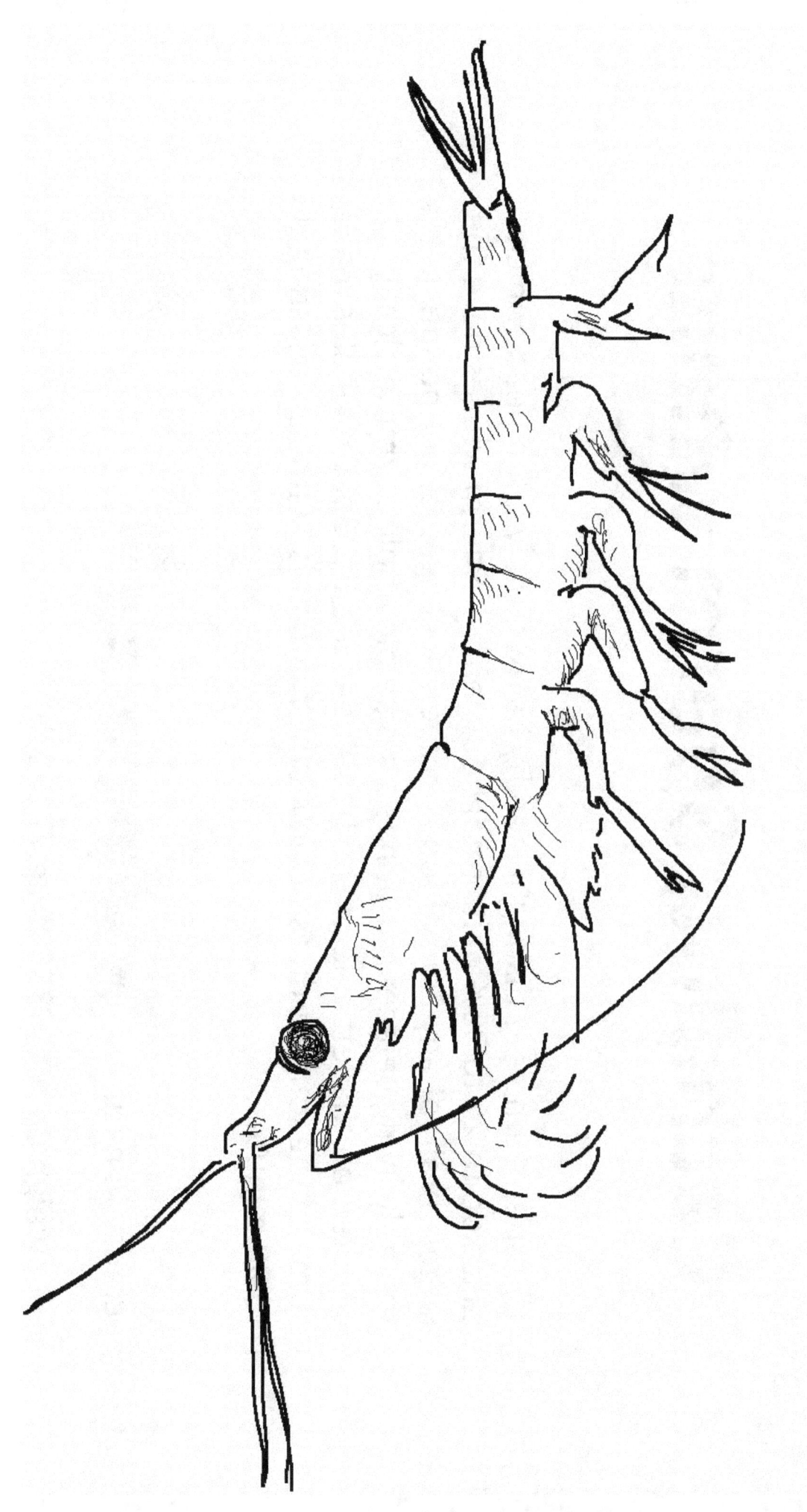

Cachalot, Sperm whale

The sperm whale is distinguished by its extremely large head, which takes up to 25 to 35% of its total body length. Sperm whales have the largest brain of any animal (on average 7.8 kilograms (17 pounds). It is the only living cetacean that has a single blowhole asymmetrically situated on the left side of the head near the tip. Sperm whales make some of the longest dives achieved by mammals, with some lasting up to 90 minutes.

life expectancy in nature

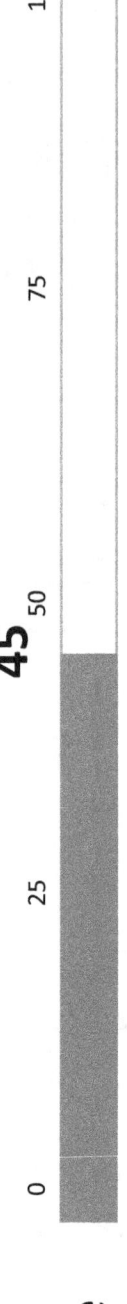

45

weigh up to   35000 kg 77100 lb)

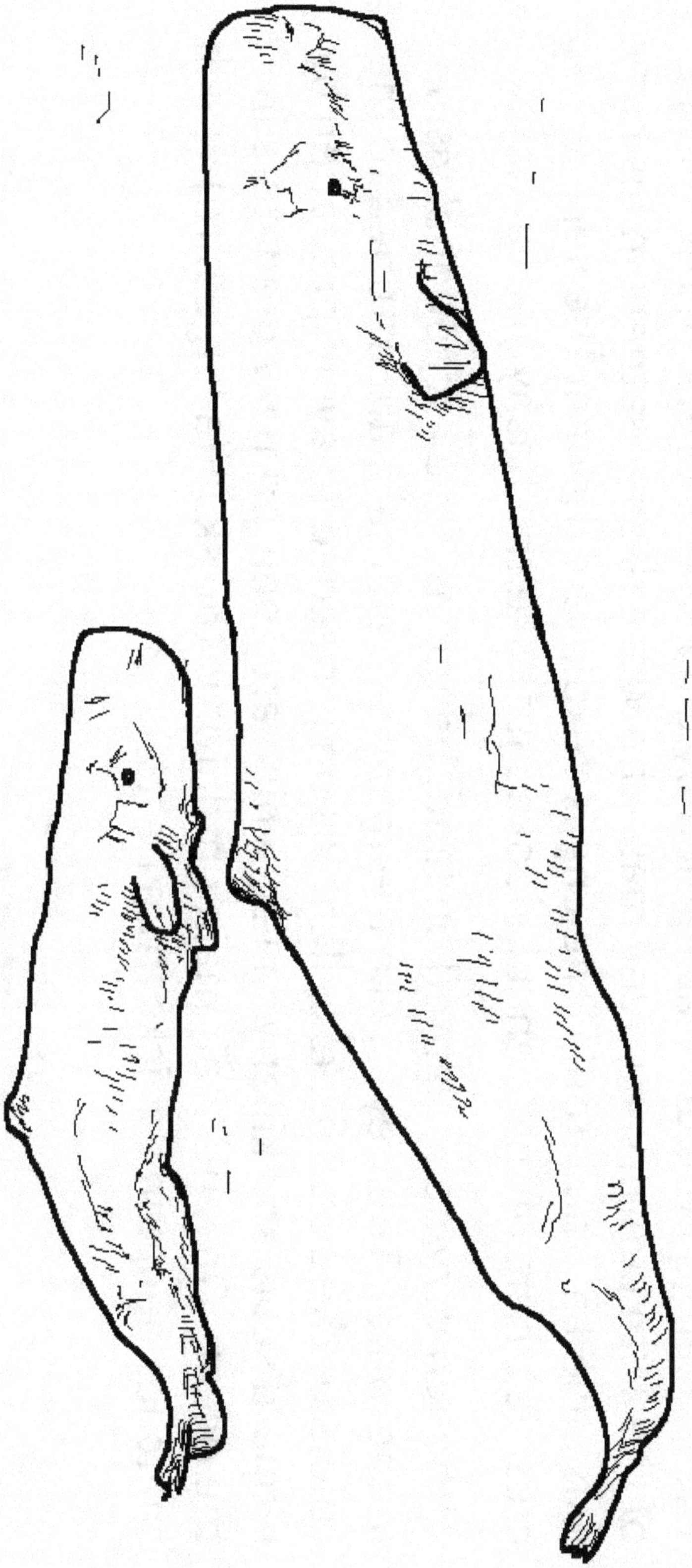

Macaroni penguin

The macaroni penguin was named by English explorers. In the middle of the 18th century, a young man who wore flashy feathers in his hat was called a "macaroni". The English explorers thought the yellow crest feathers of this penguin looked just like the flashy young man.

Although very near-sighted on land, penguins have exceptional vision in the water. Their eyes, like the many sea animals, are attuned to the colors of the sea. This excellent vision is needed to avoid predation by leopard seals and killer whales, which are their primary predators in the ocean. On land their main predator is the skua (a large bird) which snatches penguin's chicks from nests.

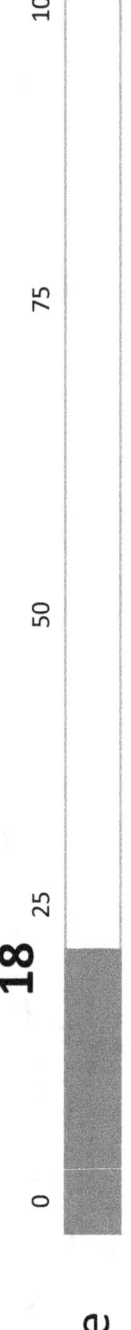

life expectancy in nature

18

weigh up to   7 kg (15 lb)

0   25   50   75   100

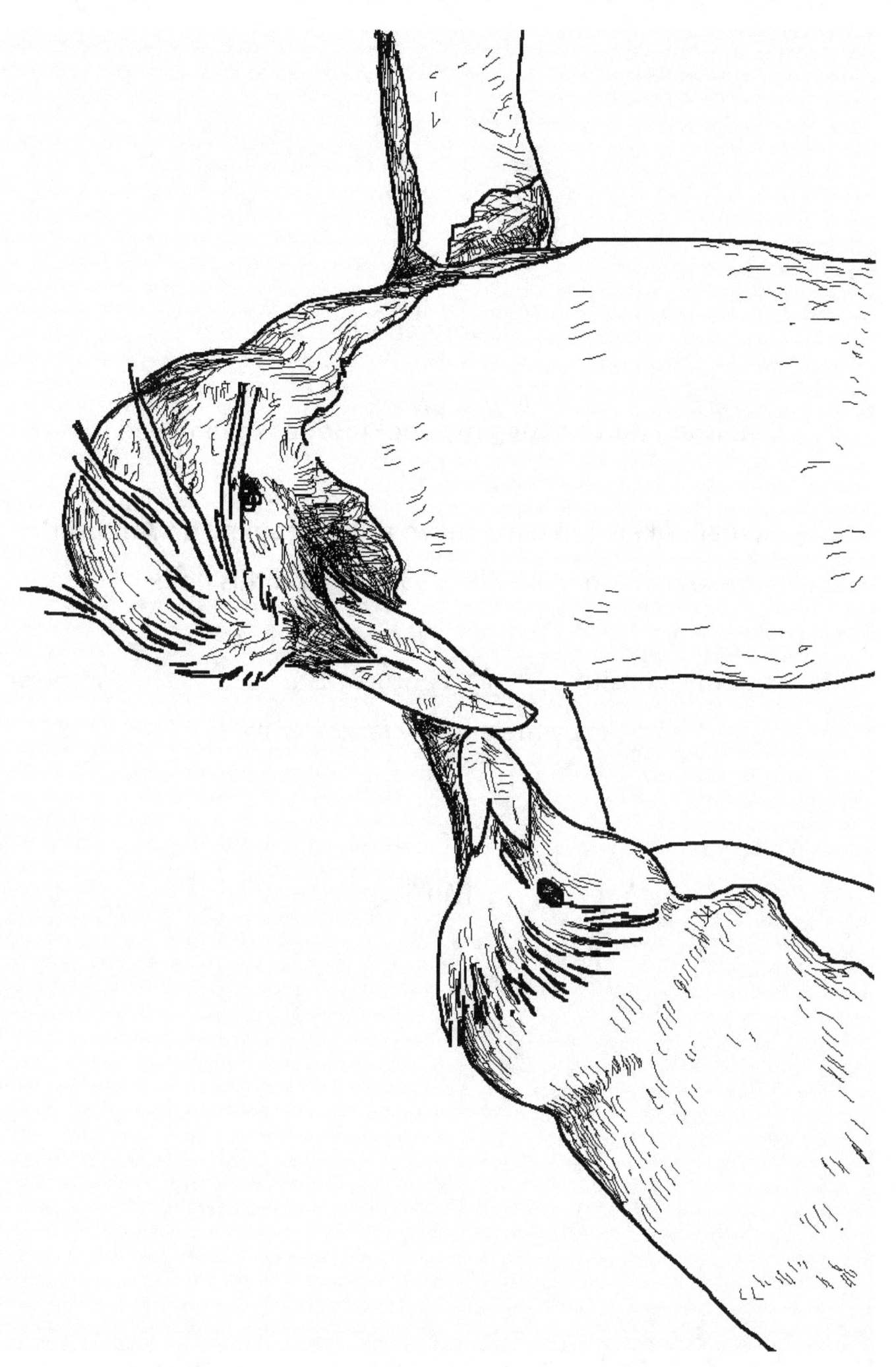

Dear Reader!

Thank you for choosing my book! Hope you enjoyed it!

If you really liked it, please, **leave a short review on Amazon!**
Use ISBN # 9781079225969 to find this book

Check out my website http://21centurywritersclub.com/ for more
books by me and my fellow writers!

See ya,
Mark

SEARCH MORE COLORING BOOKS

Book Series: Animal Planet

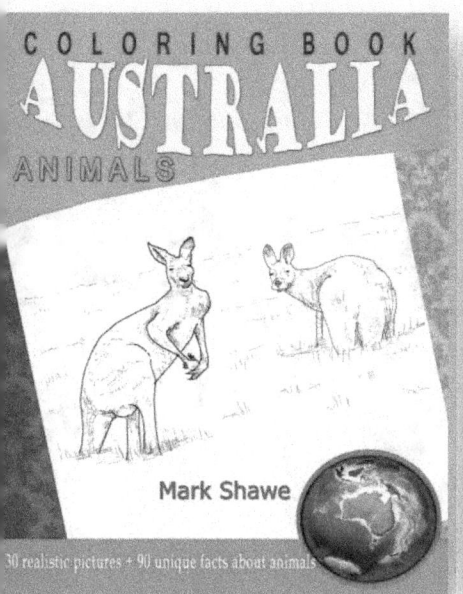

Animals of Australia

ISBN # 9781079226393

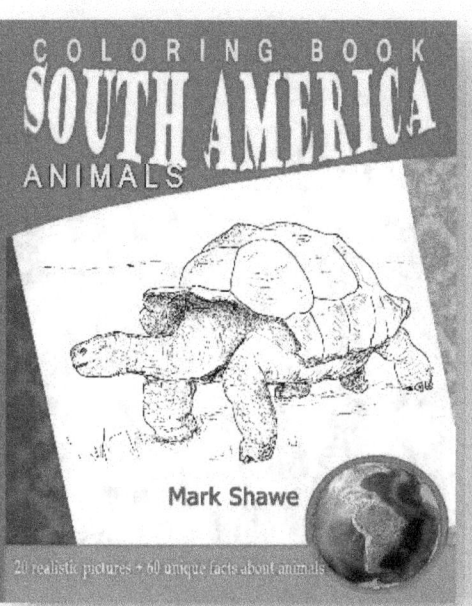

Animals of South America

ISBN # 9781079222920

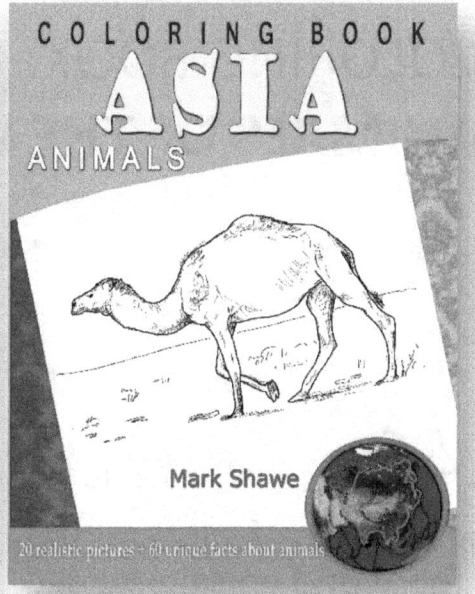

Animals of Asia

ISBN # 9781079224740

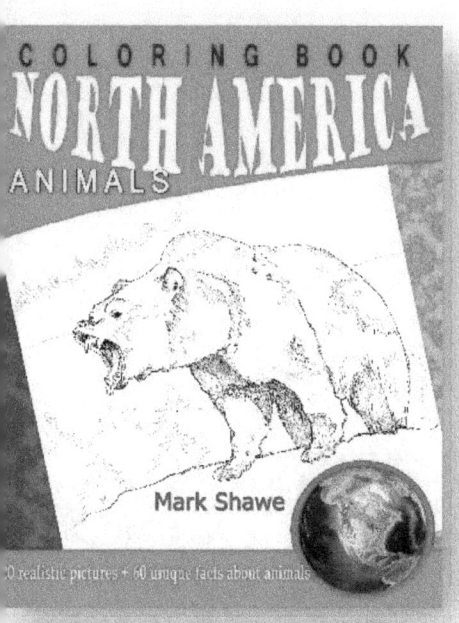

Animals of North America

ISBN # 9781079225525

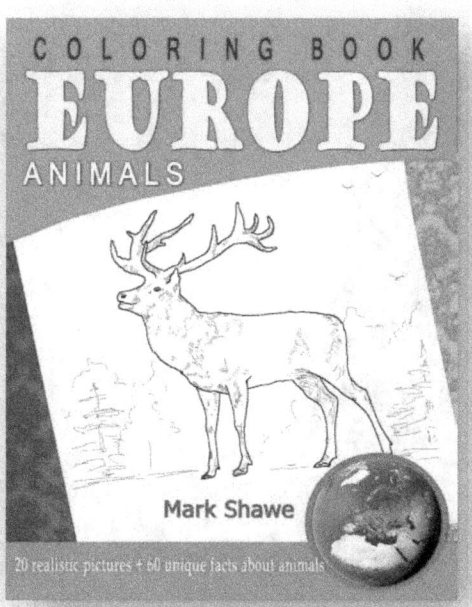

Animals of Antarctica

ISBN # 9781079222258

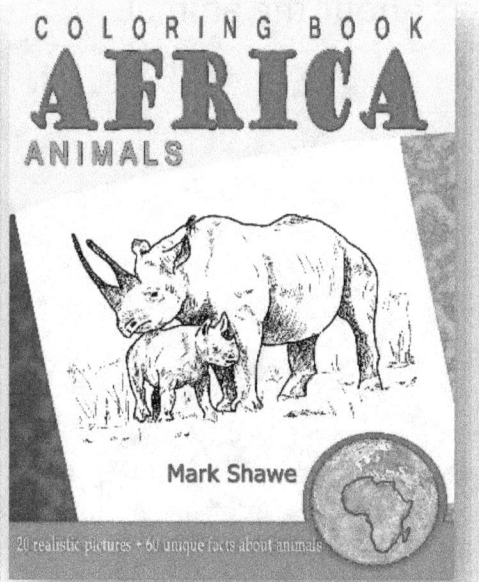

Animals of Africa

ISBN # 9781079227536

SPECIAL EDITION

COLORING BOOK:
ANIMALS OF THE WORLD

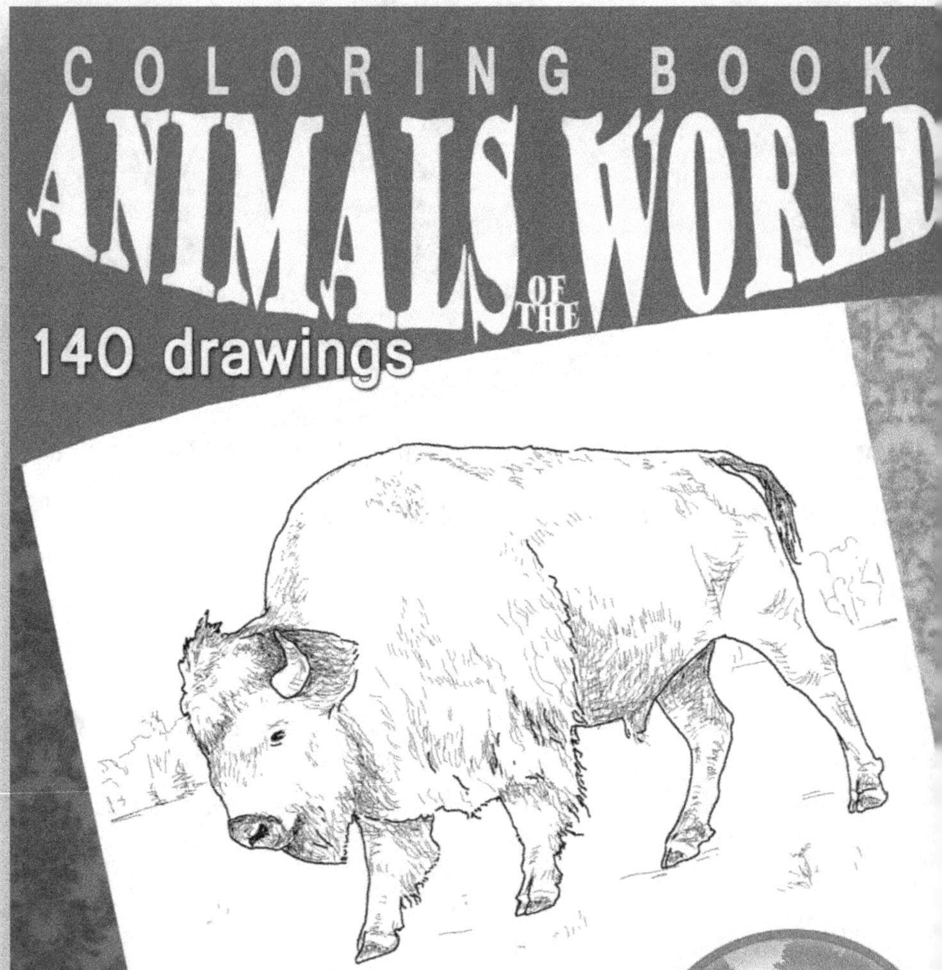

140 original realistic full-page images of wild animals of the World on single-sided sheets to prevent bleed-through

420 interesting unusual facts about the animals

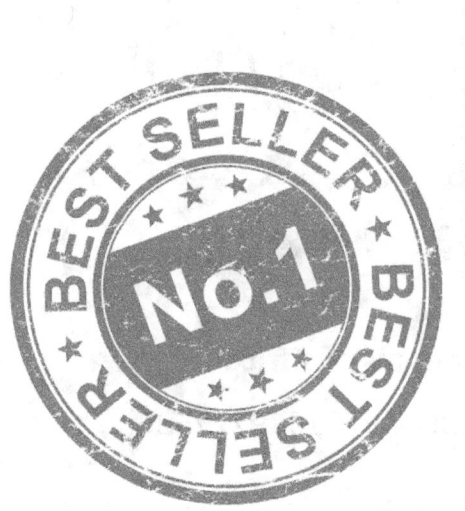

COLORING BOOK
ANIMALS OF THE WORLD
140 drawings

Mark Shawe

140 realistic pictures + 420 unique facts about animals

ISBN # 9781079226799

Book Series: **Animal Planet**